Herp Help